Teachings of OUR PROPHET

(Salla-Allāhu 'alaihi wa sallam)

A Selection of Ahādīth for Children

Elementary Level

Abidullah Ghazi
(Ph.D. Harvard)
Tasneema Khatoon Ghazi
(Ph.D. Minnesota)

IQRA' INTERNATIONAL EDUCATIONAL FOUNDATION
7450 Skokie Blvd.
Skokie, IL 60077

Part of a Comprehensive and Systematic Program of Islamic Studies

Program of Sirah
Preschool/Elementary Level

Approved By
Rabita al-Alam al-Islami
Makkah Mukarramah

Chief Program Editors
Abidullah al-Ansari Ghazi
(PhD Harvard University)

Tasneema Ghazi
(PhD University of Minnesota)

Printed in the United States of America
Fourth Printing July, 2000
Fifth Printing April, 2003

Special note on copyright:
This book is a part of IQRA's comprehensive and systematic program of Islamic Studies being developed for a planned Islamic Education of Muslim children and youth.

IQRA' International Educational Foundation
7450 Skokie Blvd., Skokie, IL 60077
tel: 847-673-4072; fax: 847-673-4095
e-mail: iqra@aol.com; website: http://www.iqra.org

ISBN # 1-56316-159-1
Library of Congress Control Number: 00-134561

بسم الله الرحمن الرحيم

IN THE NAME OF ALLĀH,
THE MERCIFUL,
THE MERCY GIVING

لَقَدْ كَانَ لَكُمْ فِي رَسُولِ ٱللَّهِ أُسْوَةٌ حَسَنَةٌ

"Indeed, in the messenger of Allah you have

beautiful example."

[al-Aḥzâb 33:21]

قُلْ إِن كُنتُمْ تُحِبُّونَ ٱللَّهَ

فَٱتَّبِعُونِي يُحْبِبْكُمُ ٱللَّهُ وَيَغْفِرْ لَكُمْ ذُنُوبَكُمْ

"Say (O Muhammad to all human kind), if you love Allah follow me, Allah will love you and forgive you your sins."

[Äl 'Imran 3:31]

CONTENTS

IQRA'S NOTE:

Teachings of our Prophet, an anthology of *aḥâdîth* is specially prepared for our young readers as enrichment literature in Iqra's *Program of Sirah*. Being the teachings of our Prophet (S) its message, value and usefulness is for all age groups - and must be studied by all.

The book provides eighty one *Aḥâdîth* specially selected for young readers.Its vocabulary is controlled and difficult words are given in the glossary at the end of the book. Each *Hadîth* is written in Arabic, translitrated, translated in simple English and explained.When this anthology is utilized as part of our *Program of Sirah*,best results may be expected.

The student is recommended to memorise the *Ḥadîth* and its meaning. Teachers/Parent may read the explanation with children and further explain the significance of each *Ḥadîth*. A story from the Iqra's *Stories of the Sirah* or *Sirah* collection may further illustrate the message of the *Hadîth*. Iqra' plans to prepare manuals for teachers soon.

The teachers are recommended to read one or two *Aḥâdîth* with each lesson of *Our Prophet* (Textbook) or *Mercy to Mankind* and ask children to read it aloud at least ten times and preferably memorise. Special recognition may be given to those children who memorise most *Aḥâdîth*.

We recommend parents and teachers to familiarise themselves with our new anthology *Guidance from the Messenger* for Junior/Senior level and utilize this in teaching the *Sirah* at various levels.

This second revised edition incorporates some comments and opinions we received. We are happy to improve the authenticity and usefulness of this book with your assistance.

We need your cooperation, participation and *Du'â* in Iqra's continuing pioneering efforts for Islamic education.

INTRODUCTION

Allah (*Subḥanhu wa Ta'âla*) sent Rasulullah (*Salla Allâhu 'alaihi wa Sallam*) as His last prophet and messenger.

He sent His last book the Qur'an to Rasulullah (S) through the angel Jibrîl (*'Alaihi as-Salâm*). The words of the Qur'an and its teachings are safegauarded by Allah (SWT). The message of the Qur'an is for the entire human beings and for all time to come.

Rasulullah (S) taught us the teachings of the Qur'an and showed us how to follow them. Allah (SWT) made Rasulullah (S) as the beautiful model for our life. Allah (SWT) says in the Qur'an:

لَقَدْ كَانَ لَكُمْ فِي رَسُولِ ٱللَّهِ أُسْوَةٌ حَسَنَةٌ

"INDEED, IN THE MESSENGER OF ALLAH YOU HAVE BEAUTIFUL EXAMPLE."
[al-Aḥzâb 33:21]

And further the Qur'an says:

"And indeed, you (O Muhammad) are of exalted character."
[Al-Qalam 68:4]

Umm al-Mu'minîn 'Aishah (*Radhi Allâhu 'anha*) said about Rasulullah (S): "His morals were the Qur'an."

Rasulullah's life was the teachings of the Qur'an in practice. Rasulullah (S) taught us how to lead our life according to the teachings of the Qur'an. His conduct is called the *Sunnah*. Rasulullah's *sunnah* is the best model for us to follow.

Allah (SWT) asked us to follow Rasulullah (S),

قُلْ إِن كُنتُمْ تُحِبُّونَ ٱللَّهَ فَٱتَّبِعُونِى يُحْبِبْكُمُ ٱللَّهُ وَيَغْفِرْ لَكُمْ ذُنُوبَكُمْ

"Say (O Muhammad to all human kind), if you love Allah follow me, Allah will love you and forgive you your sins."
[Äl 'Imran 3:31]

To be worthy of the love of Allah (SWT) we must follow the teachings of

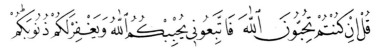

Rasulullah (S). His conduct is the best to follow. His morals are most beautiful.

Saḥâbah of Rasulullah (S) and early Muslims recorded the teachings of Rasulullah (S) and this literature is called *Ḥadîth*. There are several collections of *Aḥâdîth* (plural of *Ḥadîth*).

Each *Ḥadîth* starts with the name of a narrator and the words of "*Qâla Qâla* Rasulullah (S)" i.e. "It is said that Rasulullah (S) said." Then there is a chain of names called *Isnâd* which tells us the names of the narrators of the *Ḥadîth*.

Not all the *aḥâdîth* are of equal value. There are some which are most reliable. There are others which are less reliable. There are some which are just made up. There is a whole science of *Hadîth* and the scholars who master this science are called *Muḥaddithûn* (singular *Muḥaddith*). They are experts who look at *Ḥadîth* text (*Matn*) and the line of narrators (*Isnâd*) to find out how authentic the *Ḥadîth* is.

In this collection we have selected only eighty one *Aḥâdîth* which teach us about some aspect of Islam. Some of the selected

Aḥâdîth are not complete, they are part of longer *Aḥâdîth*. The number of *Aḥâdîth* is kept small and text short to enable you to memorise them and understand their meaning and message.

There is no good in learning *Ḥadîth* without practicing it. To practice a *Ḥadîth* means to follow the teachings and *Sunnah* of Rasulullah (S). It also means to be a good Muslim and a model human being. May Allah help us to follow the *Sunnah* of Rasulullah (S) and make us worthy of His love.

Let us study these *Aḥâdîth* and see how noble are the teachings of Rasulullah (S).

☆ *INTENTION* ☆

إِنَّمَا ٱلْأَعْمَالُ بِالنِّيَّاتِ

Innamal a‘mālu bin-niyyāti

★ ★ ★

Actions are governed by intention.

(al-Bukhārī, Muslim)

★ ★ ★ ★ ★

All actions must be performed to please Allāh. Allāh rewards a good action if it is inspired by a good intention. If we try to do something good but are unable to do so, Allāh is still pleased and rewards us for our good intentions.

★ ★ ★ ★ ★ ★ ★

This is the first part of the Hadith which continues on the next page.

☆ *REWARD FOR INTENTION* ☆

وَ إِنَّـــمَا لِكُلِّ ٱمْـــرِئٍ مَّـا نَـــوَىٰ

Wa innamā likulli imri'im mā nawā

★ ★ ★

Everyone is rewarded for what he intended.

(al-Bukhārī, Muslim)

★ ★ ★ ★ ★

Allāh rewards us according to our intentions. If by Allāh's will, our good intentions lead to unfavorable results, we will still be rewarded for our good intentions. Allāh's help will always be with us in all our actions.

★ ★ ★ ★ ★ ★ ★

☆ *ISLĀM* ☆

أَسْلِمْ تَسْلَمْ

Aslim Taslam

★ ★ ★

Accept Islām and you will be saved.

(al-jāmi' aṣ-Ṣaghīr)

★ ★ ★ ★ ★

Accepting Islam saves one from the evils of this world and from the fire of Hell in the Hereafter. Islam is a straight path which leads us to the best of both the worlds. Allāh rewards Muslims for their faith and action.

★ ★ ★ ★ ★ ★ ★

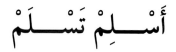

☆ *AD-DĪN* ☆
(THE RELIGION)

أَلدِّيْنُ يُسْــــرٌ

Ad-Dīnu yusrun

★ ★ ★

The religion of Islam is easy.

(al-Bukhārī)

★ ★ ★ ★ ★

Islam's teachings are simple and easy to follow. Islam does not require us to give up our family or property. Islam does not allow us to torture our body and deny ourselves all comforts. Islam is a natural and balanced way of life.

★ ★ ★ ★ ★ ★ ★

☆ *NAṢĪḤAH* ☆
(ADVICE)

أَلدِّيْـــنُ النَصِيْـحَـــة

Wa innamā likulli imri'im mā nawā

★ ★ ★

The religion (Islam) is a sincere advice.

(al-Bukhārī)

★ ★ ★ ★ ★

Islam guides all human beings to Allāh's path. Muslims wish well for all people. Therefore, they should present Islam as good advice to everyone. As sincere advice helps a person in the difficulties of life, so does Islam help him in the difficulties of both the worlds.

★ ★ ★ ★ ★ ★ ★

☆ *DA'WAH* ☆
(INVITATION)

أُدْعُــــوا ٱلنَّـــاسَ

Ud'ūn nāsa

★ ★ ★

Invite others to Islam.

(Muslim)

★ ★ ★ ★ ★

Every Muslim has a duty to present Islam's teachings to Muslims and non-Muslims alike. There are no churches or priests in Islam, and every individual is a *Dā 'ī* of Islam. We can invite others to Islam through our speech and pen, but the best way of *Da 'wah* is to practice Islam and show it through practical example.

★ ★ ★ ★ ★ ★ ★

☆ THE COMMUNITY ☆

يَـدُ اللهِ مَـعَ ٱلْـجَـمَاعَـةِ

Yadullāhi ma'al jamā'ati

★ ★ ★

Allāh's hand is with the community.

(at-Tirmidhī)

★ ★ ★ ★ ★

Muslims are one community. They should always live their lives as an organised community. Allāh protects and supports them when they live as one community. When Muslims start fighting in the name of race, language, origin, Allāh withdraws his favors. The Muslims then become an easy prey to their enemies. Muslims must always remain united.

★ ★ ★ ★ ★ ★ ★

☆ *UNITY OF UMMAH* ☆

اَلْجَمَاعَةُ بَرَكَةٌ

Al-jamā'atu barakatun

★ ★ ★

The Community is blessed.

(Abū Dā'ūd)

★ ★ ★ ★ ★

Islam does not teach us to work only for our own good and to think only of ourselves. A Muslim lives in a society and considers the interests of all. A community based on Islamic beliefs has the support and blessing of Allāh.

★ ★ ★ ★ ★ ★ ★

☆ *DISLIKE* ☆

لاَ تَنَافَرُوْا

Lā tanāfarū

★ ★ ★

Do not fight each other.

(Muslim)

★ ★ ★ ★ ★

Unity is important among friends, relations, and community. Fighting is destructive; it breaks apart friendships and family members and interferes with Islamic brotherhood. We should search for peaceful ways to handle our differences. We must learn to respect other peoples' rights and opinions.

★ ★ ★ ★ ★ ★ ★

☆ *SHAHĀDAH* ☆
(DECLARATION OF FAITH)

مِفْتَاحُ ٱلجَنَّةِ شَهَادَةُ أَنْ لَا اِلٰهَ اِلَّا اللهُ

Miftāḥul jannati shahādatu an lā ilāha illallāhu

★ ★ ★

Declaring that "there is no God but Allāh"
is the key to Paradise *(Jannah).*

(Aḥmad)

★ ★ ★ ★ ★

To believe in Allāh alone as our Lord and in no other god or power is *Tawḥīd*. Recognizing Allāh as one's Lord prevents him from the worship of idols, animals, trees, and stars. It makes him see the truth of Islam. *Shahādah* unlocks the doors of Paradise as a key unlocks the doors of our homes.

★ ★ ★ ★ ★ ★ ★

☆ *ṢALĀT : THE PILLAR OF FAITH* ☆

اَلصَّلٰوةُ عِمَادُ اَلدِّيْنِ

Aṣ-Ṣalātu ʻimādud dīni

★ ★ ★

Ṣalāt is the pillar of the religion of Islam.

(at-Tabrānī)

★ ★ ★ ★ ★

Five daily prayers are obligatory for all adult Muslims. As a building is supported by strong pillars, our faith is supported by *Ṣalāt.* If one does not offer *Ṣalāt* his house of faith will be in ruins.

★ ★ ★ ★ ★ ★ ★

☆ *ṢALĀT : KEY TO PARADISE* ☆

مِـفْـتَاحُ ٱلجَـنَّـةِ ٱلصَّـلٰوةُ

Miftāḥul jannati Aṣ-Ṣalātu

★ ★ ★

Ṣalāt **is the key to Paradise.**

(Aḥmad, Ibn Mājah)

★ ★ ★ ★ ★

Five daily prayers are *Fard* (obligation) upon all adult Muslims. No one may enter Paradise without maintaining his five daily prayers. Thus, *Ṣalāt* is a key which opens the locked doors of Paradise to a Believer.

★ ★ ★ ★ ★ ★ ★

☆ *JAMĀʻAH* ☆
(CONGREGATION)

عَلَيْكُمْ بِالْجَمَاعَةِ

ʻAlaikum bil jamāʻati

★ ★ ★

Offer *Ṣalāt* with *Jamāʻah* (congregation).

(Nisāʼī)

★ ★ ★ ★ ★

Offering *Ṣalāt* in *Jamāʻah* is a *Sunnah*. Its reward is twenty-seven times more than saying *Ṣalāt* individually. Even when there are only two people, they should offer *Ṣalāt* together in *Jamāʻah*. Islam wants to unite people through the worship of one God.

★ ★ ★ ★ ★ ★ ★

☆ *ṢAWM* : A *SHIELD* ☆ (FASTING)

أَلصَّــومُ جُنَّــةٌ

Aṣ-Ṣawmu junnatun

★ ★ ★

The *Ṣawm* is a shield (against all sins).

(Nisā'ī and at-Tirmidhī)

★ ★ ★ ★ ★

Fasting in the month of Ramadan is obligatory upon all adult Muslims. *Ṣawm* purifies our bodies and souls, brings us closer to Allāh, cleans our sins and protects us from future sins. Thus *Ṣawm* protects us from evil thoughts and actions, as a shield protects a warrior from attacks.

★ ★ ★ ★ ★ ★ ★

☆ *ZAKĀT* ☆

أَدُّوا ٱلزَّكٰوةَ

Adduz-Zakāta

★ ★ ★

Pay *Zakāt*.

(al-Baihaqī)

★ ★ ★ ★ ★

Zakāt is a *Fard* (obligation) for every Muslim who has wealth in excess of a certain quantity. Thus, a rich Muslim is required to share his wealth with the poor. A Muslim society is a brotherhood of faith. We must share with others what Allāh has blessed us with.

★ ★ ★ ★ ★ ★ ★

☆ ḤAJJ ☆ (PILGRIMAGE)

أَلحَــجُّ جِــهَادٌ

Al-Ḥajju jihādun

★ ★ ★

Ḥajj (Pilgrimage) is (a kind of) *Jihād*.

(Ibn Mājah)

★ ★ ★ ★ ★

Performing *Ḥajj* once in lifetime is an obligation upon any Muslim who can afford it. *Jihād* means struggling and sacrificing in the way of Allāh. In *Ḥajj*, we struggle with our money and body, and sacrifice our comfort to please Allāh.

★ ★ ★ ★ ★ ★ ★

☆ *DU‘Ā’* ☆
(PRAYER)

اَلدُّعَاءُ مُخُّ ٱلْعِبَادَةِ

Ad-Du‘ā’u mukhkhul ‘ibādati

★ ★ ★

Du‘ā’ **(prayer) is the kernel of the *‘Ibādah*** **(worship).**

(at-Tirmidhī)

★ ★ ★ ★ ★

The *‘Ibādah* (worship) brings us closer to Allāh. Through *Du‘ā’* (prayer) we ask for Allāh’s favors and forgiveness for our mistakes. Allāh loves those who turn to Him in their need and ask Him for His favors.

★ ★ ★ ★ ★ ★ ★

☆ *DHIKR* ☆ (REMEMBERING)

أَلذِّكْرُ نِعْمَــةٌ

Adh-Dhikru niʿmatun

★ ★ ★

The *Dhikr* of Allāh is a blessing.

(ad-Dailamī)

★ ★ ★ ★ ★

It is a blessing to remember Allāh. His presence in our mind brings us peace and joy. *Dhikr* keeps us away from both evil thought and bad actions. It helps us to do the right things.

★ ★ ★ ★ ★ ★ ★

☆ *TAWBAH* ☆
(REPENTANCE)

أَلنَّدَمُ تَوْبَةٌ

An-nadamu tawbatun

★ ★ ★

Remorse of sin is repentance.

(*Jawāmi'*)

★ ★ ★ ★ ★

Tawbah does not mean only saying words of repentance but true *Tawbah* is the feelings of sorrow in our hearts. When we sincerely accept our mistakes and turn to Allāh, He forgives us.

★ ★ ★ ★ ★ ★ ★

☆ ASK FORGIVENESS ☆

تُوبُوْا إِلَى اللهِ وَاسْتَغْفِرُوْهُ

Tūbū ilallāhi wastaghfirū hu

★ ★ ★

Repent to Allāh and ask for His forgiveness.

(Muslim)

★ ★ ★ ★ ★

We as human beings make mistakes both intentionally and unintentionally. We should constantly ask for Allāh's forgiveness. Allāh loves those who turn to Him with pure hearts and He opens the doors of His mercy upon them.

★ ★ ★ ★ ★ ★ ★

☆ *MASJID : THE BEST PLACE* ☆

أَحَبُّ ٱلْبِلَادِ إِلَى اللهِ مَسَاجِــدُهَا

Aḥabbul bilādi ilallāhi masājiduhā

★ ★ ★

The best places in the sight of Allāh are the *Masājid*.

(Muslim)

★ ★ ★ ★ ★

The *Masājid* (pl. of *Masjid*, mosque) are places to remember Allāh. When we are in a *Masjid*, we read the Qur'ān, offer *Ṣalāt* and think of Allāh. When we are outside the *Masjid*, there are many distractions which destroy our purity of thought.

★ ★ ★ ★ ★ ★ ★

☆ *SALĀM ON RASŪLULLĀH (S)* ☆

مَنْ صَلَّى عَلَيَّ مَرَّةً
صَلَّى اللهُ عَلَيهِ عَشراً

Man Ṣalla ʻalayya marratan
ṣallallāhu ʻalaihi ʻasharan

★ ★ ★

One who sends Allāh's blessings upon me once, will be blessed ten times by Allāh.

(al-Bukhārī, Muslim)

★ ★ ★ ★ ★

Allāh loves His Prophet (S), and He loves those who love His Prophet (S). When we send Salām to Rasūlullāh (S), Allāh is pleased and rewards us with His blessings ten times.

★ ★ ★ ★ ★ ★ ★

☆ *PROPHET : A TEACHER* ☆

اِنَّـــمَا بُعِثْتُ مُعَلِّـــماً

Innamā bu'ithtu mu'alliman

★ ★ ★

I was sent as a teacher.

(Ibn Mājah)

★ ★ ★ ★ ★

Rasūlullāh (S) did not know how to read or write, but Allāh gave him the Qur'ān and taught him its meaning and made him a teacher for all mankind.

★ ★ ★ ★ ★ ★ ★

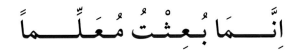

☆ *MUḤAMMAD'S MISSION* ☆

بُعِثْتُ لِأُتَمِّمَ مَكَارِمَ الْأَخْلاقِ

Bu'ithtu li utammima makārim al-akhlāqi

★ ★ ★

I have been sent to perfect good morals and manners.

(Aḥmad)

★ ★ ★ ★ ★

Allāh sent Rasūlullāh (S), as a mercy and the best model for all mankind. His morals and manners are the best example for everyone to follow. He showed us in practice what Islam teaches us.

★ ★ ★ ★ ★ ★ ★

☆ *HIS MORALS AND MANNERS* ☆

كَانَ خُـلُـقُـــهُ ٱلْقُـــرْآنَ

Kāna khuluqu hul Qur'āna

★ ★ ★

His morals and manners were the Qur'ān.

(al-Bukhārī)

★ ★ ★ ★ ★

Umm ul-Mu'minīn, 'Āishah (R) related this Hadīth. She said that Rasūlullāh's life was a practical example of the Qur'ānic teachings. What the Qur'ān taught, Rasūlullāh practiced.

★ ★ ★ ★ ★ ★ ★

☆ THE QUR’ĀN ☆

تَعَاهَدُوا الْقُرْآنَ

Ta‘ah-hadul Qur’āna

★ ★ ★

Take good care of the Qur’ān.

(Agreed Upon)

★ ★ ★ ★ ★

Taking good care of the Qur’ān means reading, reciting, memorizing, learning and understanding its message. It also means teaching the Qur’ān to others and inviting everyone to the truth of the Qur’ān.

★ ★ ★ ★ ★ ★ ★

☆ TEACHING THE QUR'ĀN ☆

خَيْرُكُمْ مَنْ تَعَلَّمَ ٱلْقُرْآنَ وَعَلَّمَهُ

Khairu kum man ta'allamal Qur'āna wa 'allamahu

★ ★ ★

The best person among you is the one who learns the Qur'ān and teaches it to others.

(al-Bukhārī, Muslim)

★ ★ ★ ★ ★

Both learning and teaching the Qur'ān are important. We must learn the Qur'ān and teach others to read and benefit from it. The teachings of the Qur'ān are for everyone. We have a duty to make the message of the Qur'ān known to the entire world.

★ ★ ★ ★ ★ ★ ★

☆ *LEARNING : OBLIGATORY* ☆

طَلَبُ ٱلْعِلْمِ فَرِيْضَةٌ عَلَىٰ كُلِّ مُسْلِمٍ وَمُسْلِمَةٍ

Ṭalabul ʻilmi farīḍatun ʻalā kulli
Muslimin wa Muslimatin

★ ★ ★

Seeking knowledge is *Farḍ* upon every
Muslim man and Muslim woman.

(Ibn ʻĀdī)

★ ★ ★ ★ ★

Every Muslim man and woman should seek knowledge. Our Prophet (S) was a teacher. Allāh gave him His book the Qur'ān. First word of the *Waḥī* (revelation) was *Iqra'* (read). We should acquire both religious and non-religious knowledge.

★ ★ ★ ★ ★ ★ ★

☆ *KNOWLEDGE* ☆

اَلْعِلْمُ خَلِيْلُ ٱلْمُؤْمِنِيْنَ

Al-'Ilmu Khalīlul-Mu'minīn

★ ★ ★

Knowledge is a friend to the Mu'minūn (the Believers).

(al-Baihaqī)

★ ★ ★ ★ ★

True friends support us and help us in our needs. Knowledge is a true friend of the *Mu'minūn* because it aids them in both this world and the Hereafter. The knowledge helps the *Believers* to make this world a better place to live in. It also helps them to work for the best in the Hereafter.

★ ★ ★ ★ ★ ★ ★

☆ *TEACHING* ☆

بَلِّغُوْا عَنِّي وَلَوْ آيَةً

Ballighū 'annī wa law āyatan

★ ★ ★

Inform others on my behalf though it may be a single verse.

(al-Bukhārī)

★ ★ ★ ★ ★

One does not have to be a scholar or priest to teach Islam. Every Muslim has a responsibility to teach others whatever he knows of Rasūlullāh's (S) message. Whatever we know of Islam we must pass on to others.

★ ★ ★ ★ ★ ★ ★

☆ SAY AS-SALĀMU ‘ALAIKUM ☆

أَلسَّلَامُ قَبْلَ ٱلْكَلَامِ

As-Salāmu qabl al-kalāmi

★ ★ ★

Say, *As-Salāmu ‘Alaikum,* before you begin speaking.

(at-Tirmidhī)

★ ★ ★ ★ ★

Whenever we see Muslims we should greet them with *As-Salāmu ‘Alaikum.* If we wish to speak to someone we should do so after greeting them. We should try to be the first to say *As-Salāmu ‘Alaikum.*

★ ★ ★ ★ ★ ★ ★

☆ *AS-SALĀMU ‘ALAIKUM* ☆

أَفْشُوا ٱلسَّلَامَ بَيْنَكُمْ

Afshus Salāma bainakum

★ ★ ★

Greet each other with *As-Salāmu ‘Alaikum*
(Peace of Allāh be with you)

(at-Tirmidhī)

★ ★ ★ ★ ★

All of us need peace and security from Allāh. The Islamic greeting and its reply are a *Du‘ā’* (prayer) for our friends and visitors. Muslim brothers and sisters return our greetings by saying, *Wa ‘Alaikum as-Salām*, (and with you be the peace of Allāh). Thus we bless one another every time we meet.

★ ★ ★ ★ ★ ★ ★

☆ *MERCY* ☆

إِرْحَمُوْا تُرْحَمُوْا

Irḥamū turḥamū

★ ★ ★

Show mercy to others and you will receive the mercy.

(al-Bukhārī, Muslim)

★ ★ ★ ★ ★

Allāh is Merciful and Mercy-giving. He rewards us when we are merciful to others. Other people are also kind to us when we show kindness to them.

★ ★ ★ ★ ★ ★ ★

☆ *GENEROSITY* ☆

أَلْجَنَّةُ دَارُ ٱلْأَسْخِيَاءِ

Al-Jannatu dārul askhiyā'i

★ ★ ★

Paradise is the home of the generous.

(Abū Dā'ūd)

★ ★ ★ ★ ★

People who give their wealth to the poor and needy, and for other good causes such as building a *Masjid*, hospital or school, will be rewarded with Paradise as their home in the Hereafter.

★ ★ ★ ★ ★ ★ ★

☆ *SINCERITY* ☆

إِخْلِصِ الْعَمَلَ

Ikhliṣil ʻamala

★ ★ ★

Have sincerity in your actions.

(al-Baihaqī)

★ ★ ★ ★ ★

Many people do good deeds to show others, to gain social prestige and position. Our intentions should be to please Allāh alone. When we do things to please Allāh alone, Allāh rewards us both in this world and the Hereafter.

★ ★ ★ ★ ★ ★ ★

☆ *TRUTH* ☆

عَلَيْكُمْ بِالصِّدْقِ

'Alaikum biṣ-ṣidqi

★ ★ ★

Be truthful.

(at-Tirmidhī)

★ ★ ★ ★ ★

One should always speak the truth. No one trusts or respects a person who tells lies. A truthful person is successful because people trust him, and are ready to accept what he says.

★ ★ ★ ★ ★ ★ ★

☆ *TRUST* ☆

أَلأَمَانَـــةُ عِـــزٌّ

Al-Amānatu ʻizzun

★ ★ ★

True honor lies in keeping one's trust.

(ad-Dailamī)

★ ★ ★ ★ ★

A Muslim should be honest and trustworthy. Everyone respects a person who inspires trust. In Makkah, Rasūlullāh (S) was known as *al-Amīn,* the trustworthy. Muslims must follow the teachings of their religion and the example of their Prophet (S).

★ ★ ★ ★ ★ ★ ★

☆ *Ḥ*AYĀ' (MODESTY) ☆

اَلْـحَـيَاءُ خَـيْرٌ كُـلُّـهُ

Al-Ḥayā'u khairun kulluhu

★ ★ ★

Everything about modesty is good.

(Muslim, Abū Dā'ūd)

★ ★ ★ ★ ★

A modest person is respected and trusted by everyone. People know a modest person does not seek anything unlawful. He speaks nicely and helps others. He respects the privacy of his friends and neighbors. Rasulullah (S) said "Everything about modesty is good". It can also be said that everything about immodesty is bad.

★ ★ ★ ★ ★ ★ ★

☆ *MODESTY* ☆

أَلْـحَـيَاءُ شُعْبَـةٌ مِنَ ٱلإِيْـمَـانِ

Al-Ḥayā'u shu'batum minal īmāni

★ ★ ★

Modesty is a part of faith.

(Muslim)

★ ★ ★ ★ ★

Ḥayā' means modesty. A believer must be modest in behaviour and in every walk of his life. He must show his modesty in his walk, talk, dress, and general behaviour. Modesty is an important sign of one's faith.

★ ★ ★ ★ ★ ★ ★

☆ *PROMISE* ☆

لاَ دِيْـنَ لِـمَنْ لاَ عَـهْـدَ لَـهُ

Lā dīna liman lā ʻahda lahū

★ ★ ★

A person who does not keep his promise has no religion.

(Ibn an-Najjār)

★ ★ ★ ★ ★

Allāh wants Muslims to fulfill their promises. Many people say *Insha Allāh* when making a promise, when their intention is not to fulfill that promise. This kind of promise is even worse. A person who does not keep promises is like one who has no faith in Allāh and the Hereafter.

★ ★ ★ ★ ★ ★ ★

☆ *AL-KADHIB* ☆
(LYING)

أَلْكَذِبُ مُجَانِبُ ٱلإِيْمَانِ

Al-Kadhibu mujānibul Īmāni

★ ★ ★

A lie weakens *Īmān* (faith).

(ad-Dailamī)

★ ★ ★ ★ ★

Real faith means truthfulness under every condition. The habit of lying creates a distance between liars and their faith. The more one lies, the weaker his *Īmān* becomes, and finally a liar loses his faith altogether.

★ ★ ★ ★ ★ ★ ★

☆ *LYING AND LIVELIHOOD* ☆

أَلْـكَـذِبُ يَـنْـقِــصُ ٱلرِّزْقَ

Al-Kadhibu yanqiṣur rizqa

★ ★ ★

Lying reduces one's livelihood.

(Musnad Aḥmad)

★ ★ ★ ★ ★

People who lie are disliked and mistrusted and have difficulty finding a good position. Sometimes lying might bring them temporary gains, but those gains are eventually lost. When people discover someone's lies, they do not trust that person and avoid him.

★ ★ ★ ★ ★ ★ ★

☆ *ḤASAD* ☆
(JEALOUSY)

إِيَّـاكُمْ وَٱلْـحَسَـدَ

Iyyākum wal ḥasada

★ ★ ★

Save yourself from *Ḥasad*.

(Abu Dā'ūd)

★ ★ ★ ★ ★

Ḥasad (jealousy) is one of the worst weaknesses of human beings. A jealous person burns with hatred when he sees another's happiness or success. A jealous person may sometimes harm others, but he will always harm himself.

★ ★ ★ ★ ★ ★ ★

☆ *HATRED* ☆

لاَ تَبَاغَضُوْا

Lā tabāghaḍū

★ ★ ★

Do not hate eath other.

(al-Bukhārī)

★ ★ ★ ★ ★

Hatred is like a disease which destroys the hater more than it harms others. Hatred is often returned with hatred and creates mistrust. It destroys relationships and friendships. It destroys the whole society.

★ ★ ★ ★ ★ ★ ★

☆ ANGER ☆

إِجْتَنِبُوْا ٱلْغَضَبَ

Ijtanibul ghaḍaba

★ ★ ★

Avoid anger.

(al-Qarshī)

★ ★ ★ ★ ★

When we are angry, we lose control over our judgement and language. When angry we often say and do things which we may later regret.

★ ★ ★ ★ ★ ★ ★

☆ *FITNAH : MISCHIEF* ☆

إِيَّـاكُمْ وَٱلْفِـتْـنَــةَ

Iyyākum wal fitnata

★ ★ ★

Save yourself from mischief.

(Ibn Mājah)

★ ★ ★ ★ ★

Fitnah means mischief which creates enmity among people and disorder in society. The Qur'ān says "*fitnah* is worse than killing". A *Fitnah* may lead to quarrel, enmity, hatred, and war. The whole society suffers because of *Fitnah*.

★ ★ ★ ★ ★ ★ ★

☆ *GHĪBAH* ☆
(BACKBITING)

إِيَّاكُمْ وَٱلْغِيْبَةَ

Iyyākum wal ghībata

★ ★ ★

Save yourself from *Ghībah*.

(Abū Shaikh)

★ ★ ★ ★ ★

Ghibah is one of the worst vices in Islam. The Qur'ān says that *Ghibah* is like eating the flesh of your dead brother. How mean a person who eats the flesh of his dead brother. Of course, no one can really do it, but one does *Ghibah*, which is worse than eating flesh of one's dead brother.

★ ★ ★ ★ ★ ★ ★

☆ *WORSE THAN KILLING* ☆

اَلْغِيْبَةُ أَشَدُّ مِنَ ٱلْقَتْلِ

Al-Ghībatu ashaddu minal qatli

★ ★ ★

Ghībah **is worse than killing someone.**

(ad-Dailamī)

★ ★ ★ ★ ★

A backbiter attacks other people's characters when they aren't even there to defend themselves. A person if killed innocent, is a *shahīd* and goes to *Jannah.* A person whose character is attacked often finds it hard to face society. That is why Rasulullah (S) said that attacking someone's character is worse than killing him.

★ ★ ★ ★ ★ ★ ★

☆ *KHIYĀNAH* ☆
(CHEATING)

إِيَّاكُمْ وَٱلْخِيَانَةَ

Iyyākum wal khiyānata

★ ★ ★

Save yourself from *Khiyānah* (cheating).

(Ṭabarānī)

★ ★ ★ ★ ★

Khiyānah means cheating, falsehood, disloyalty, betrayal and deception. A *Khā'in* (cheater) loses respect in the eyes of Allāh and is mistrusted by his fellow human beings.

★ ★ ★ ★ ★ ★ ★

☆ SPYING ☆

لاَ تَجَسَّسُوْا

Lā tajassasū

★ ★ ★

Do not spy upon people.

(al-Bukhārī)

★ ★ ★ ★ ★

Everyone has the right to privacy. We should respect this right and resist spying or nosiness. Those people who spy on others also spread rumours. Spying and spreading rumours creates bad feelings and in the end, spoils good relationships.

★ ★ ★ ★ ★ ★ ★

☆ *SHOW OFF* ☆

أَلـرِّيَــاءُ شِرْكٌ

Ar-Riyā'u shirkun

★ ★ ★

Showing off is equal to *Shirk*.

(Baihaqī)

★ ★ ★ ★ ★

Riyā' is a good action which one performs to show off for people and not to please Allāh. *Riyā'* is as bad as *Shirk* (accepting partners with Allāh). Our desire to please Allāh should be the sole reason for our actions.

★ ★ ★ ★ ★ ★ ★

☆ FALSE ACCUSATIONS ☆

لاَ يَدْخُلُ ٱلْجَنَّةَ مُفْتَرٍ

Lā yadkhulul jannata muftarin

★ ★ ★

One who makes false accusations will not enter Heaven.

(ad-Dailamī)

★ ★ ★ ★ ★

Falsely accusing innocent people is a great sin. The innocent person does not know how to defend himself. Many people start believing the accuser. It causes a lot of embarrassment and pain for the accused. That is why a false accuser will never enter Paradise.

★ ★ ★ ★ ★ ★ ★

☆ *YOUR TONGUE* ☆

إِحْــفَـظْ لِـسَانَــكَ

Iḥfaz lisānaka

★ ★ ★

Safeguard your tongue.

(*Ibn Asākir*)

★ ★ ★ ★ ★

Muslims should safeguard their tongues from evil speech such as lying, backbiting, slandering, swearing, etc. We should also be careful not to lose control over ourselves when we are angry. While angry, people often say things which they later regret.

★ ★ ★ ★ ★ ★ ★

☆ *ENJOIN GOOD* ☆

أَلـدَّالُّ عَـلَىٰ ٱلْـخَـيْرِ كَـفَاعِـلِـهِ

Ad-Dāllu 'alal khairi kafā'ilihī

★ ★ ★

One who encourages others to do good deeds is like one who performs them.

(al-Jāmi' aṣ-Ṣaghīr)

★ ★ ★ ★ ★

Those who invite others to do good deeds get reward from Allāh for their work. A good moral society can not be made if only a few practice good while others continue to do evil. We should always invite others to do good deeds.

★ ★ ★ ★ ★ ★ ★

☆ *KHULUQ* ☆
(BEST MANNERS)

أَحْسِنْ خُـلُـقَكَ لِلـنَّاسِ

Aḥsin khuluqa ka lin-nāsi

★ ★ ★

Treat others with the best manners.

(Mālik)

★ ★ ★ ★ ★

A Muslim's faith is shown by the way he or she treats others. In Islam, *Khuluq* (moral behavior) is as important as inner feelings. A Muslim must show others his Islamic faith through his good actions.

★ ★ ★ ★ ★ ★ ★

☆ THE BEST PERSON ☆

خَيْرُ ٱلنَّاسِ أَنْفَعُهُمْ لِلنَّاسِ

Khairun nāsi anfa'uhum lin nāsi

★ ★ ★

The best person is one who benefits other people.

(Mināwī)

★ ★ ★ ★ ★

The best person in the sight of Allāh is not one who has wealth or position but one who serves mankind. A Muslim must help everyone, Muslim and non-Muslim alike. Muslims should be known for their kindness, courtesy, and help to others.

★ ★ ★ ★ ★ ★ ★

☆ *THE PIOUS* ☆

أَكْـرَمُ ٱلنَّـاسِ أَتْـقَـاهُـــمْ

Akramun nāsi atqā hum

★ ★ ★

The most respected among people are those who are most pious.

(al-Bukhārī, Muslim)

★ ★ ★ ★ ★

Allāh honors those who are pious and act righteously. The pious fear Allāh and treat other human beings with love and respect. Their fellow men, in turn, respect and love them.

★ ★ ★ ★ ★ ★ ★

☆ TRUE ROOTS ☆

أَلْـحَسَـبُ أَعْـمَـالٌ

Al-Ḥasabu a'mālun

★ ★ ★

True nobility of a family is its good actions.

(Aḥmad)

★ ★ ★ ★ ★

Islam teaches that the true test of a person's nobility is his deeds and not his family, birthplace, race or color. Rasūlullāh (S) taught us that a noble person is one whose actions are noble. A noble family is one whose members perform noble deeds.

★ ★ ★ ★ ★ ★ ★

☆ *KARAM : TRUE NOBILITY* ☆

كَرَمُكُمْ تَقْوٰكُمْ

Karamu kum taqwā kum

★ ★ ★

Your true nobility is in your *Taqwā.*

(al-Dailamī)

★ ★ ★ ★ ★

Taqwā means piety, righteousness and obedience to Allāh's commands. In Islam, true nobility is not in wealth, position, color or race, but rather in one's piety and good character. The Qur'ān says "the most noble person in the eyes of Allāh is he who has *Taqwā* (most).

★ ★ ★ ★ ★ ★ ★

☆ *SELF RESPECT* ☆

أَلْـمُـؤمِـنُ يَـغَـارُ

Al-Mu'minu yaghāru

★ ★ ★

The Mu'min (Believer) has self-respect

(Muslim)

★ ★ ★ ★ ★

Sometimes people sacrifice their honor and principles to gain small benefits from others. Believers have self-respect because they know that Allāh is the only Provider and Helper. They do not sacrifice their Islamic principles and self-respect for wordly gains.

★ ★ ★ ★ ★ ★ ★

☆ *ḤALĀL EARNINGS* ☆

كَسْبُ ٱلْـحَـلَالِ فَـرِيْـضَــةٌ

Kasbul ḥalāli farīḍatun

★ ★ ★

Striving for a *Ḥalāl* livelihood is an obligation.

(Baihaqī)

★ ★ ★ ★ ★

Every Muslim must work for a *Ḥalāl* living. Unlawful earnings are completely forbidden. There may be some temporary gains in Haram earnings, but for Muslims there is no *Barakah* in Haram earnings in this world and in the *Akhirah*.

★ ★ ★ ★ ★ ★ ★

☆ *EYEWITNESS* ☆

لَيْسَ ٱلْخَبَرُ كَالْمُعَايَنَةِ

Laisal khabaru kal mu'āyanati

★ ★ ★

Second hand information is not like first hand observation.

(Muslim)

★ ★ ★ ★ ★

Any information received by others can not be the same as seeing it ourselves. We must verify second hand news rather than believing it immediately. Thus we can avoid spreading false information and rumors.

★ ★ ★ ★ ★ ★ ★

☆ *DEBT* ☆

إِيَّـــاكُمْ وَالـدَّيْـــنَ

Iyyākum wad daina

★ ★ ★

Avoid going into debt.

(Baihaqī)

★ ★ ★ ★ ★

One should only borrow money when in great need. The debts should always be repaid as soon as possible. The habit of borrowing keeps a person permanently in debt. He lives beyond his means and may many times lose his property to lenders. He also does not have peace of mind.

★ ★ ★ ★ ★ ★ ★

☆ *EXCHANGE GIFTS* ☆

تَـهَادُوْا تَـحَابُّـــوْا

Tahādū taḥābū

★ ★ ★

**Exchange gifts with each other,
you will love each other.**

(al-Bukhārī, Muslim)

★ ★ ★ ★ ★

Giving gifts shows our love and concern for others. It also creates our love and concern in the hearts of those who receive them. The exchange of gifts is, in fact, an exchange of our good feelings for each other. Thus it increases love and respect for each other.

★ ★ ★ ★ ★ ★ ★

☆ *SILENCE IN ANGER* ☆

إِذَا غَضِبَ أَحَدُكُمْ فَلْيَسْكُتْ

Idhā ghadiba aḥadukum fal yaskut

★ ★ ★

When you feel angry, keep silent.

(Muslim)

★ ★ ★ ★ ★

Remaining silent when in anger can stop us from saying bad things. It also helps us to control our anger. Anger leads us to bad situations which could be embarrassing or dangerous.

★ ★ ★ ★ ★ ★ ★

☆ *DISEASE* ☆

لِـكُـلِّ دَاءٍ دَوَاءٌ

Li kulli dā'in dawā'un

★ ★ ★

There is a cure for every disease.

(Abū Dā'ūd)

★ ★ ★ ★ ★

As Allāh created disease, He also provides a cure. Rasūlullāh (S) taught us to consult doctors and take medicine when we are sick. Muslim scientists have the responsibility of trying to find a cure for every disease through research and experiment.

★ ★ ★ ★ ★ ★ ★

☆ *BAD OMEN* ☆

اَلطِّيَرَةُ شِـــرْكٌ

Aṭ-Ṭīratu shirkun

★ ★ ★

To believe in a bad omen is *Shirk*.

(*Aḥmad*)

★ ★ ★ ★ ★

Allāh controls everything. No omen is good or bad. Accepting an omen or superstition is like accepting an authority beside Allāh. A Muslim knows that only Allāh knows the future. We trust Allāh and leave everything to him.

★ ★ ★ ★ ★ ★ ★

☆ *TAHĀRAH* ☆
(CLEANLINESS)

أَلطَّهَارَةُ شَطْرُ الْإِيْمَانِ

Aṭ-Ṭahāratu shaṭrul-īmāni

★ ★ ★

***Tahārah* is half of one's faith.**

(at-Tirmidhī)

★ ★ ★ ★ ★

A Muslim must have a pure soul and a clean body. *Waḍū* (ablutions) and *Ghusl* (bath) keep one's body clean and fresh. A Muslim must also wear clean clothes. He should always avoid unclean habits.

★ ★ ★ ★ ★ ★ ★

☆ BORROWED THINGS ☆

أَلْعَارِيَةُ مُؤَدَّةٌ

Al-'Āriyatu mu'addatun

★ ★ ★

A borrowed thing should be returned.

(al-Kanz)

★ ★ ★ ★ ★

When we borrow things from friends and neighbors, we should take them back as soon as we have finished using them. It is the duty of a borrower to return things to the lender in good condition and promptly.

★ ★ ★ ★ ★ ★ ★

☆ *FEED OTHERS* ☆

أَطْعِمُوْا ٱلْجَائِعَ

At'imul jā'i'a

★ ★ ★

Feed the hungry.

(Abū Dā'ūd)

★ ★ ★ ★ ★

There are many people in the world who are hungry and have no food to eat. It is the duty of all Muslims to share their food and money with the hungry and needy. We can feed the hungry directly or we can contribute to charities which help the hungry and the needy.

★ ★ ★ ★ ★ ★ ★

☆ *NEIGHBOR* ☆

لِجَارِكَ عَلَيْكَ حَقٌّ

Li jārika ʿalaika ḥaqqun

★ ★ ★

Your neighbor has rights over you.

(Kanz, ad-Dailamī)

★ ★ ★ ★ ★

Islam teaches us to be kind and helpful to our neighbors. It is not enough just to love our neighbors, we must show our love through our actions. Neighborhood sometimes creates hostility and jealousy. Bad relations with neighbors hurt and harm everyone. Rasulullah (S), therefore taught us to be extra kind to our neighbors.

★ ★ ★ ★ ★ ★ ★

☆ *ḤALĀL* ☆
(LAWFUL)

طَلَبُ ٱلْحَلَالِ جِهَادٌ

Ṭalabul ḥalāli jihādun

★ ★ ★

Seeking a *Ḥalāl* livelihood is a *Jihād*.

(Abū Nu'aim)

★ ★ ★ ★ ★

Earning one's living lawfully, through honest labour, is a struggle in the way of Allāh. There are many ways to make easy money. Burglary, cheating, usury and other illegal ways make it easy for us to get rich. A believer always seeks *Halāl* means though he may have to lead a hard life.

★ ★ ★ ★ ★ ★ ★

☆ *SERVE MOTHERS* ☆

اَلْـجَـنَّـةُ تَحْتَ أَقْـدَامِ ٱلأُمَّـهَاتِ

Al-Jannatu taḥta aqdāmil ummahāti

★ ★ ★

Paradise lies under the feet of mothers.

(Muslim)

★ ★ ★ ★ ★

We should humble ourselves before our mothers. Through serving them with humility, we earn Allāh's pleasure and paradise. Before you go to sleep tonight, ask yourself, "What have I done to please my mother today?".

★ ★ ★ ★ ★ ★ ★

☆ *DRINKING* ☆

إِشْرَبُوْا ٱلْـمَـاءَ بِعُـيُـوْنِـكُمْ

Ishrabul mā' bi 'uyūnikum

★ ★ ★

Examine water before you drink it.

(Muslim)

★ ★ ★ ★ ★

We must examine water before drinking it to make sure that it is clean. Rasūlullāh (S) advised us to keep water and food covered. Dust or small insects pollute water and it endangers our health.

★ ★ ★ ★ ★ ★ ★

☆ *EATING* ☆

بِسْمِ اللهِ ، وَكُلْ بِيَمِيْنِكَ

Bismillāhi wa kul bi yamīnika

★ ★ ★

Begin with Bismillah and eat with your right hand.

(al-Bukhārī, Muslim)

★ ★ ★ ★ ★

Muslims should start everything by saying *Bismillāhir Raḥmānir Raḥīm*. We should eat with the right hand since the left hand is used for cleaning.

★ ★ ★ ★ ★ ★ ★

☆ *INTOXICANTS* ☆

كُــلُّ مُسْكِرٍ حَــرَامٌ

Kullu muskirin ḥarāmun

★ ★ ★

Every intoxicant is *Ḥarām* (forbidden).

(al-Bukhārī)

★ ★ ★ ★ ★

All intoxicants, alcohols, and drugs (besides medicines), are harmful to our body. They take away our judgement and lead us to perform immoral, illegal and dangerous actions. A Muslim should always maintain control of his mind and body.

★ ★ ★ ★ ★ ★ ★

☆ DU'Ā' : BEFORE EATING ☆

أَللّٰهُمَّ بَارِكْ لَنَا فِيْمَا رَزَقْتَنَا
وَقِنَا عَذَابَ ٱلنَّارِ بِسْمِ اللهِ

Allāhumma bārik lanā fīmā razaqtanā
wa qinā 'adhāban nāri, bismillāhi

★ ★ ★

O Allāh! bless the food that You have given us,
save us from punishment of Fire and
start eating with the name of Allāh.

(Shamā'il at-Tirmidhī)

★ ★ ★ ★ ★

When you start eating, say this *Du'ā'* and start eating with your right hand.

★ ★ ★ ★ ★ ★ ★

☆ DU'Ā' : AFTER EATING ☆

أَلْحَمْدُ لِلّٰهِ ٱلَّذِىْ أَطْعَمَنَا وَ سَقَانَا
وَجَعَلَنَا مِنَ ٱلْمُسْلِمِيْنَ

Al Ḥamdu lillāhil ladhī at'amanā wa saqānā
wa j'al-nā minal Muslimīna

★ ★ ★

All praises are due to Allāh who gave us
to eat and to drink and made us Muslims.

(Shama'il at-Tirmidhī)

★ ★ ★ ★ ★

When you finish eating say this *Du'ā'*.

★ ★ ★ ★ ★ ★ ★

☆ *DU'Ā' : ENTERING THE MASJID* ☆

أَللّٰهُمَّ ٱفْتَحْ لِىْ أَبْوَابَ رَحْمَتِكَ

Allāhumma iftaḥli abwāba raḥmatika

★ ★ ★

O Allāh! open the doors of
your *Raḥmah* (mercy) for me.

(Muslim)

★ ★ ★ ★ ★

Upon entering the *Masjid,* put your right foot inside the door and say this *Du'ā'*.

★ ★ ★ ★ ★ ★ ★

☆ *DU‘Ā’ : LEAVING THE MASJID* ☆

أَللّٰهُمَّ إِنِّي أَسْئَلُكَ مِنْ فَضْلِكَ

Allāhumma innī as’aluka min faḍlika

★ ★ ★

O Allāh! I ask you to give me your *Faḍl*
(kindness and generosity).

(Muslim)

★ ★ ★ ★ ★

Upon leaving the *Masjid,* put your left foot outside the door and say this *Du‘ā’*.

★ ★ ★ ★ ★ ★ ★

☆ *DU‘Ā’ OF FATHER* ☆

دُعَاءُ ٱلْوَالِدِ لِوَلَدِهِ كَدُعَاءِ ٱلنَّبِيِّ لِأُمَّتِهِ

Du‘ā’ul wālidi li waladihī kadu‘ā’in
nabiyyi li ummatihī

★ ★ ★

Father's *Du‘ā'* (prayer) for his son is as acceptable to Allāh as a prophet's prayer for his *Ummah.*

(ad-Dailamī)

★ ★ ★ ★ ★

A prophet's main concern is his *Ummah*, just as a father's main concern is his children. When we please and obey our parents, they will ask Allāh to bless us. Allāh listens to their prayers as He listens to the prayers of His Prophets. Every child should try to earn the *Du‘ā’* (prayer) of his or her parents.

★ ★ ★ ★ ★ ★ ★

GLOSSARY

al-Amin	trustworthy, title of prophet Muhammad (S)
Barakah	blessings
borrower	who borrows
community	Ummah, group of people
church	Christian institution. A building for worship
Da'i	one who gives *Da'wah* (invitation) of Islam.
deception	misleading, tricking
distraction	diversion, taking attention away from something
Du'a	prayer to Allah
embarrassing	distressing, confusing
eventually	finally, at least
fard	obligation, duty
forgiveness	pardon
Ghîbah	backbiting
Halâl	permissible under Islamic law, legal
Hereafter	life after death
humble	modest, without pride
Harâm	not permissible under Islamic law, illegal
humility	modesty, lack of pride
immodesty	not proper in behavior, dress, or speach, prentitious
inspire	to influence someone to do something
intentionally	with intention, or purpose
intoxicant	alcohol, wine, drugs which produce intoxication

Iqra'	read, recite, proclaim
Jama'ah	congregation, group, party
judgement	decision
manners	behaviour, habitual conduct
memorise	to learn by heart
message	teachings, instructions
mission	task, *da'wah* work
morals	knowledge of right and wrong
(to) motivate	to inspire, to influence
kernel	inside of seed that people eat such as almound, walnut etc.
Khulûq	morals, manners
obligation	fard, duty
observation	to watch something carefully
omen	sign
permanently	forever
pious	one of right conduct, God fearing
principles	rules
remorse	regret for past mistake or sin
repent	asking for forgiveness of past sin, to make Tawbah
repentance	Tawbah
responsibility	to be answerable for a duty
righteous	someone doing what is right
righteousness	act of doing right
(to) ruin	(to) destroy

Riya	doing things for show, showoff
sacrifice	to forego something for others to please Allah
scholar	a person with great knowledge
security	freedom from risk
Shahâdah	to declare one's faith in Allah and His Messenger, martyrdom
social prestige	respect in society
superstition	belief not accepted by reason or religion
Tahârah	cleanliness and purification according to Islamic law
Tawbah	repentance
temporary	for a short time
torture	to put someone in pain
unfavourable	not helpful
unintentionally	without intention, or purpose